Building Biblical Worldview

The Three Loves

Joe Neff, ThM

D1403230

Rooted Schools, LLC
Little Rock, Arkansas 72211
www.rootedschools.org

©2016 Joe Neff
Published by Rooted Schools, LLC
27 Perdido Circle, Little Rock, AR 72211
RootedSchools.org

Details in some anecdotes and stories have been changed to protect the identities of the persons involved.

Unless otherwise indicated, Scripture taken from the NEW AMERICAN STANDARD BIBLE®, Copyright © 1060, 1962, 1963, 1968, 1971, 1972, 1973, 1975, 1995 by The Lockman Foundation. Used by permission.

Copies of this book may be purchased at a discount for quantities, with special interest in helping the book be available for Christian school leaders and teachers. Contact RootedSchools.org. Workshops, courses, ebooks, and other resources are available to help teachers grow in The Three Loves. See BuildingBiblicalWorldview.com.

ISBN-13: 978-0997282405
ISBN-10: 0997282401

1. Christian education 2. Biblical Worldview 3. Christian schools 4. Bible 5. Love

ACKNOWLEDGEMENTS

Thanks to Dr. Darrell Smith for his encouragement to pursue writing about the "Sweet Spot" of the three loves.

And, to the faculty of Little Rock Christian Academy for being good eggs when I experimented with ideas like this. I am blessed to have seen the three loves in the lives of many.

CONTENTS

PREFACE

Thank you for taking a look at *Building Biblical Worldview: The Three Loves.* I hope you find something in it useful for you and your situation. I think you will.

I am convinced that integrating faith and learning, the historic call to Christian schools, is best done with a biblical worldview. A biblical worldview in every subject draws students to Jesus and their subjects, and sees how to look at life and live it through God's eyes.

This is why Christian schools exist, how we are different.

In *Building Biblical Worldview: The Three Loves* you will find a model for creating great biblical worldview that has worked. The exciting part for me: it isn't complicated, but goes straight to a simple concept from God's Word. A simple concept large enough to change the world.

The model is practical. It can be implemented anywhere. It provides a foundation that lasts and can grow with attention to specific steps.

The model is inexpensive. Any school, rich or poor, can use it. Where there is a cost, it is probably less than money spent on other professional development.

The model is powerful. Because it is an application of the living Word of God, it impacts lives. And, it is strong enough to support any specific doctrine or concepts that a school uses.

I hope it works for you. And, if not, that it will help you think about how you approach biblical worldview and prod us all to better ways.

Blessings.

Joe Neff, ThM

WHY BIBLICAL WORLDVIEW

The value of biblical worldview becomes clear when we look at not only its role in Christian school education and where we are today, but what biblical worldview is and does.

This section explores those three: where we are, where we have been, and what biblical worldview is and does.

Then, we can understand why creating and sustaining biblical worldview is so important as a distinction of Christian school education and as a value for parents and students. A value that impacts lives for God's glory and purposes.

1. The Challenge for Biblical Worldview

Not long ago, the main water line between my house and the street leaked. Bad for the water bill. To make things worse, the pipe goes uphill under forty-four steps with terraces and four story high trees.

I have done some plumbing and thought about it, but this was big. It needed a serious Plumber, one with a capital P.

American Leak Detection came and quickly found the leak, thankfully in one of two places that was not buried by mounds of earth and tall trees. A blessing.

Their plumbers came back a few days later to fix it. The two men had a white panel van with big doors showing racks of tools and parts. They dug a hole, found a bad joint, and repaired the leak. They added a new regulator to make things even better, sealed it up, and piled dirt back. They were in and out in eighty minutes. Good work with a lower price than estimated.

I was impressed with the stuff in the truck. It was stocked with things they might normally need, including a new regulator—who would have thought they had one of those along? And, all of their shovels, pipe cutters, saws, and many things I can't name.

They also brought their training and experience. And, they brought the good name of their company (I had checked reviews online), and a year guarantee. They even brought little booties to wear in my house.

Plumbing Beauty

The Plumbers were professionals, equipped and trained. They did the job well and made me a happy customer. They had what they needed in equipment, training, and experience. And, a great attitude and personal relationship skills. They actually seemed to have fun fixing my leak.

What they did in the muddy hole that day was a thing of beauty, workmen in their sweet spot.

We are after the same sweet spot for teachers creating a biblical worldview. Where skill, tools, training, experience, attitude, and personal relationships converge. Teachers in their sweet spot, making class a thing of beauty and giving students a special experience as they learn deeply and with joy about the subject and God, and how the two meet. Teaches with a capital T.

How do we make sure this great biblical worldview happens, every day, in every class, for every student? Even when the hole is muddy, to find pleasure and profit, and walk away with everyone saying joyfully, "well done."

The Christian School Distinctive

Since the beginning of Christian school education, biblical worldview in all subjects has been our distinctive. Biblical worldview—or as some call it, Christian worldview—is what makes us unique, different than other schools.

It is our most prized value for students and families. It is why we exist.

But, sometimes the prize evades our grasp. We get our hands around it for a moment and it slips out. We can't seem to hold it long enough to figure out how to make great biblical worldview happen all of the time, or even hold on long enough to describe it well.

How do we get a grip on this biblical worldview so we can understand it enough to replicate it in all subjects all of the time, for every student? This thing of beauty, which makes possible real integration of faith and learning.

We have some great tools and some awesome teachers. We provide books and training and guest speakers to support biblical worldview. We often have our classes in some pretty good looking buildings and rooms, too. And, we have faculty, staff, and parents who seriously want a biblical worldview.

In business terms, biblical worldview is our most significant and distinct value proposition, what a parent and student gains by coming to our school that sets us apart. When done well, we give families something that isn't just different than other schools, but beyond them.

How do we deliver this value consistently? How do we help children see God in every subject and all of life, with joy and power?

The Land to Take

I am haunted by words from Frank Gaebelein, words from a lecture at Dallas Theological Seminary in 1952 that later became *The Pattern of God's Truth*:

"When it comes to the application of the noble principles upon which it is built, Christian education in America has much to learn. We have had a great deal to say about God-centered, Christ-oriented, Bible-based education. But in actual practice we are not doing nearly enough of it….That is not to say, of course, that we are not to any extent practicing Christian education. That is too extreme a judgment. Nevertheless, in respect to a thorough-going integration of Christ and the Bible with the whole institution, with all departments of study, with all kinds of student activities, with all phases of administration, there remains much land to be taken." (BMH Books, 1954, 1968, pages 15 and 16.)

We still have land to take. We have done some great things and there are extraordinary pockets of powerful integration. But, even with some great generals and tacticians since the middle of the last century, we have not taken the mountain. And as each generation of teachers relieves those in the front lines, we can never let up our enlistment and training.

It is even hard just to hold the line and not go backward.

Planting our Flag

This is what *Building Biblical Worldview: The Three Loves* is about. A model to create and sustain powerful biblical worldview. A fundamental approach that I have seen work in classrooms and might be of use to others.

Your school may be creating consistent and powerful biblical worldview in all subjects, or at least you are further along than many of us. I sincerely hope so, and hope that this small work will simply encourage you to speak up and share your wisdom. We have teachers who are doing biblical worldview well, perhaps they or those who watch them can contribute to a bigger discussion to help all of us.

Creating discussion and sharing the good things we are doing is one of my hopes from this piece.

While looking for answers, I saw some amazing teachers along the way who seemed almost supernaturally carried along as they taught with passion and wisdom, and students experienced and learned a rich biblical worldview and excitement for the subject. Students were engaged, and we all knew these were special.

Perhaps your experience has been like mine. I have seen some of these amazing moments in the classroom. But, I have also seen sincere and hardworking teachers struggle to engage students in a rich and powerful biblical worldview, often because they don't know how, don't have the time, or don't feel they have permission. Sometimes it is just the daily battle of meeting life's needs and handling the distractions that are so much a part of school life. Every teacher I know wants to have joy and success in the battle.

Things are not bad. We do a good job with biblical content, especially in Bible or Worldview classes. We have some great teachers doing amazing things in the classrooms, helping students learn better than most other schools. This is not a critique related to the world's standards for education, we are solid there.

It is simply a question. How do we take the mountain and plant our flag? What questions do we need to ask and answer to transform and achieve powerful biblical worldview in every classroom, every time? What can you hang your hat on, every time?

My dream is for us together to fulfill Frank Gaebelein's challenge when he said that "there remains much land to be taken" in creating true biblical worldview. What Gaebelein said then still holds true today: "We have had a great deal to say about God-centered, Bible based education. But in practice we are not doing nearly enough of it."

It will only be enough when every student learns all of the time from teachers who create a powerful and rich biblical worldview.

2. What I Saw

While trying to understand how to replicate great
biblical worldview, I watched some incredible teachers
who held every student the entire class, eyes and minds
locked, and in the end those students saw the subject in
fresh ways through God's eyes.

I saw students drawn to the awesomeness of God and
the subject. Students walked out changed, at least a
little, and certainly not able to say, "That was boring."
They often carried the conversation to the next class or
home. Actually answering mom or dad when asked,
"What did you learn in school today?"

I saw something special in some classrooms where
teacher, and God, and student, and subject met. And
created something powerful. A biblical worldview that
drew students to God, to life with Him, to the subject
in life, and to learning.

But, great biblical worldview certainly did not happen in all of the classes I saw. Those where it did not happen and those where it did happen had the same tools, the same resources, and the same training. What was different?

A Special Two

In particular, I remember two amazing classes. One was a Chemistry class with juniors. The teacher passionately described the chemical aspects of purifying water, and went on to show how applications of a simple process could provide water for millions around the world. All in the context of the awesomeness and heart of God.

The other was a mock class presented for some of our faculty by a guest from another school. He had been teaching for years and was more excited than ever, in this case about amazing new discoveries in atoms that just kept showing the depth and richness of the Creator. His enthusiasm and love for God impacted those of us watching.

I noticed that the two teachers who excited us about God and the subject shared one thing.

Now that I am looking for it, I have seen the same thing in many other teachers since. And, now when I think back about great biblical worldview teachers I have known in the past, I remember the same qualities.

What did I see?

Simply, these teachers love God, love their students, and love their subject. With passion. And, with a love that compels them to know more, to live and share real life with God, to love the way God says to love as their method, their motivation, and their message.

I bet if you have teachers whose students see God's perspective and draw closer to Him and the subject, I bet that those teachers share these same qualities, these same three loves.

They love God, students, and subject.

The Plumber, Not the Wrench

Don't be fooled by the simplicity of the three loves. Fred Rogers, "Mr. Rogers," once said that "Life is simple and deep, but we make it shallow and complicated."

So it is with love, God's way. It is simple, but extraordinarily deep and powerful. Biblical love is deep enough and strong enough to be the foundation, the rock, for biblical worldview. Practically speaking, it works.

A teacher who loves well, God's way, is the solution to creating powerful biblical worldview. When love is real in the life of a teacher, students learn about God and subject, and about life from God's perspective with joy and depth. Only one thing is strong enough for this to work all of the time.

Love, God's way.

Great biblical worldview teaching is about the Plumber, not the wrench. Without the right person holding the tools, they are worthless. A teacher who loves God, student, and subject well is ready to be trained and armed with great tools and materials, to help take the land. A teacher who doesn't love is at best inept, and at worst, dangerous, with the tools and materials.

The target of *Building Biblical Worldview: The Three Loves* is the teacher, the type of teacher who does great biblical worldview because of who they are, not because we expect it, equip them, or it is part of the curriculum. Top down isn't necessary for these teachers, a biblical worldview happens because of their love. It bubbles up and overflow naturally.

It is about the teacher first. Who he or she is and is becoming.

It is about the teacher's love for God, for student, and for subject coming together in their sweet spot. For a living and powerful biblical worldview, every day for every student.

It is possible, by God's grace and by going to love.

Five Observations

Before we dig into the heart of the model and its parts, why and how it works, here are five observations about using the three loves as the primary focus for sustaining great biblical worldview teaching.

Education is a Living Thing

My father worked for years on an assembly line at General Electric making air conditioners. Other than an occasional cover change for a different brand (the insides were the same), their job was to reproduce the same air conditioner every time. This is not what great biblical worldview does. It is not an assembly line that takes curriculum and makes sure students can replicate it.

It is a living thing.

The teacher is like a flourishing tree, heavy with fruit, that God is growing so the students learn and grow fruit, passed on then to generation after generation.

These teachers naturally pop out apples for seed and nourishment. Their students not only get the curriculum, but they get it alive and tasty and able to be shared in other lives. Dried fruit? No. Fruit that is able to give life.

It happens because of who the teacher is and is becoming. It is life to life, soil and trees, seeds and water and pruning, fruit bearing fruit. The teacher makes sure that students understand, use, and are drawn to God and their subject. From God's perspective.

Every student with this experience is changed, somehow. This is the effect Jesus had on people, everyone was changed somehow. A great teacher with a living biblical worldview does the same thing.

Unlike the assembly line, there is no a checklist that will create great biblical worldview. There are some lists here that we can use, but they just don't translate automatically into great biblical worldview.

Lists can't do those things, because great biblical worldview is alive. It lives and breathes in the teacher, in the teacher who is alive in Christ using God's Word and empowered by the Holy Spirit.

The Teacher's Life

Great biblical worldview is about life, and specifically the teacher's life.

Since biblical worldview is about life, this book is intrusive and talks about the teacher's life. We have to talk about their lives if we want great biblical worldview. It is life on life.

We all know that teaching takes more than a forty hour week. It invades life and sucks all the time it can. That is true for all teachers, but even more for the great biblical worldview teacher. The impact of a teacher comes from an entire life, everything that has led to the moment, and everything that happens round the clock.

Great biblical worldview teachers love God, love students, and love their subject. This doesn't start or end, it just is. And, it happens in the midst of their personal lives with their families, pets, homes, laundry, church, vacation, in the midst of those things with other loves they have. It is who they are, not starting and stopping when the light switch in the classroom is turned on or off.

This cost to the teacher is high. It is a slice of their lives they give, sometimes the biggest piece, to teach and do it from God's perspective and for Him. These teachers are pearls of great price, reflecting Jesus and giving themselves.

Low Cost

While the price of great biblical worldview is in some ways beyond measure, drawing from lives, ironically the cost to schools doesn't have to be much. And, for teachers who want to become great biblical worldview teachers, it often doesn't take more time or cost, just a shift of focus and approach. And, in some cases, it actually means doing less and spending less.

The three loves are within reach of all schools. A big budget isn't the answer.

Building biblical worldview means learning to love deeper and letting that love drive thoughts, ideas, and interactions. It means using the same time already used for quality planning and classroom management as other teachers, but looking at planning differently, from love and for love, a love that students see and which helps the students fall in love.

As Mark Noll says, "Thus the greatest hope for Christian learning in our age, or in any age, lies not primarily in heightened activity, in better funding, or in strategizing for tasks at hand—though all of these matters play an important part. Rather, the great hope for Christian learning is to delve deeper into the Christian faith itself. And going deeper into the Christian faith means, in the end, learning more about Jesus Christ." (*Jesus Christ and the Life of the Mind.* Eerdmans, 2011, page 22.)

Love, driving us to know Jesus better, serves students differently and shares our joy and excitement about our subject and a life with God. This is the cost. It is not expensive. Yet, it is priceless.

Choosing Trust and Trees

While there is no expensive program or book that Christian school leaders need to provide, there are decisions to make about how to use professional development time to support and grow the three loves.

And, school leaders need to decide if they can be comfortable with some ambiguity, which comes from increased differentiation in professional development. Developing and encouraging the three loves is typically different for each teacher. It is not a formula where 2 + 2 equals 4. There are things we can do, things we can expect, and ways to assess faculty. But, it isn't a clean checklist that lends itself to the same professional development experiences and results for all teachers.

This living biblical worldview moment in the classroom is the result of putting together living things. Obviously, the teacher and the students are alive. As well as God, the real and true Living God. Then you throw the Word of God which is "living and active" into the mix, and you have life touching life, life invading life, and even what was dead coming alive. Life like this can be planted and nourished, but cannot be contained or packaged. It can be fed, not formulated.

School leaders also have to decide: can we trust teachers? To take their loves and put them together for students, to grow trees bearing fruit? These are messier and harder to evaluate. We have to have teachers we trust to take what we build in their lives and watch God use them, sometimes in ways that surprise, often in ways that go well beyond the basic curriculum. We can't control all of the details, if we want life.

If we believe in the power of God's Word and the power and guidance of the Holy Spirit, and that God, teachers, and students are alive, we should expect nothing less than overflowing times when put together. This biblical worldview is living and deep and wide and high.

If, instead, we want a static, scripted learning, we can get it. Students can memorize knowledge and replicate packaged applications. By expecting only that the standards and facts be learned. But, we will miss the power and beauty of great biblical worldview teaching.

If we aim low, we will get it.

But, if we want students to know those same facts and standards and also see them alive and rich, learning beyond basics, that can happen, too. By hiring and growing faculty who love God, love students, and love their subject and are growing with joy and knowledge in those loves.

To build great biblical worldview teachers, we need to be okay with some ambiguity. We need to expect more from these teachers, not the normal. We need to trust our great teachers and be surprised at what a difference the three loves makes when given room and encouragement to grow.

Love First, Bible First

Both love and Bible must be first. Love for the why and how. Bible for the what, the truth.

We are in desperate need of faculty who know God's Word from first hand study, not from a book or what someone told them it says. A teacher will not be able to find deep love and fascination to share with students unless he or she is a student of God's Word.

Ken Gangel emphasized this need a generation ago, a time when Bible understanding was better than today: "Teachers at any level of Christian education who have not had a respectable exposure to formal study of Bible and theology should not be hired" ("Integrating Faith and Learning: Principles and Process." *Bibliotheca Sacra,* April-June, 1978).

This implies a need to know how to study the Bible, not just read about what someone else says or memorize theologies. Those are good, but each teacher has to be as Gangel said, at least an "amateur theologian." It is the joy of personal discovery of truth and application to life that gives the teacher the ability to teach with a powerful biblical worldview. There is no way to teach a biblical worldview without firsthand knowledge and joy of the Bible.

A biblical worldview in the classroom is the result of a living interaction between the teacher, the student, the subject, and God. Anything less than a living and life-giving pedagogy might be safe, but won't reach the stature and power of planting and nurturing the living Word of God. Using categories, checklists, and prescribed steps as the beginning point or primary method to help teachers create biblical worldview will be weak and powerless.

"For the word of God is living and active and sharper than any two edged sword, piercing as far as the division of soul and spirit, of both joints and marrow, and able to judge the thoughts and intentions of the heart" (Hebrews 4:12). Biblical worldview is about life. God's Word is about life.

"Remind them of these things, and solemnly charge them in the presence of God not to wrangle about words, which is useless and leads to the ruin of the hearers. Be diligent to present yourself approved to God as a workman who does not need to be ashamed, accurately handling the word of truth" (2 Timothy 2:14 and 15). May we all handle the "word of truth" accurately. And, not be useless.

Especially, if we want a real and living biblical worldview in all classes.

3. What Biblical Worldview Does

I am sure you can add and probably subtract from the list below that answers the question, "What does biblical worldview do?" And, certainly, you will have specific content and skills that go beyond this list. In general, great biblical worldview in all subjects will do the following in all areas at all ages.

Points to Jesus

In its simplicity, biblical worldview is seeing the world through God's eyes. Some call it Christian worldview instead of biblical worldview to emphasize the focus on Christ. My preference is to describe what we are doing by using the source of authoritative truth and call it "biblical worldview." "Biblical" worldview becomes a statement that we believe in the Bible as the source of authoritative truth from which truth is drawn or by which all truth is tested. A whole Bible that points to and explains Jesus.

If we call it biblical worldview, it is always with the understanding that all of Scripture points to Jesus and is only understood rightly if the Gospel of Christ is central. Jesus is the focus and the content of our study and lives, and rightfully our presentation of the biblical worldview of any subject.

Whichever term we chooses, it all points to Jesus. If it doesn't, we are missing the number one goal of biblical worldview in all subjects. And, life.

Makes the Bible Foundational

Not only must the teacher personally study and use the Bible, but biblical worldview teaching places the Bible at its foundation, a rock on which to stand instead of sandy land.

Ken Gangel had more to say about the Bible and its use, "The cardinal essential for the achievement of the integration of truth in the Christian classroom is a commitment to the authority of the Bible. It is one thing to verbalize a commitment to the inspiration of Scripture; it is quite another to accept the inerrant authority of Scripture as the centerpiece for contemporary education."

Gangel quotes Gaebelein in the same piece: " 'The sheer, unapproachable greatness of the written Word of God...to take as the center of the curriculum the one book among all the other great books to which alone the superlative 'greatest' can without challenge be uniquely applied—this is neither narrow nor naïve. Rather it is simply good judgment to center on the best rather than the second best'." ("Integrating Faith and Learning: Principles and Process." *Bibliotheca Sacra*, April-June, 1978.)

The great biblical worldview teacher knows and uses God's Word. The Book is open, always standing by as the sword in God's outfitting of the soldier. And, as "breathed out by God and profitable for teaching, for reproof, for correction, and for training in righteousness, that the man of God may be competent, equipped for every good work" (2 Timothy 3:16-17).

And, teaching with a biblical worldview is a "good work."

Pursues Truth

Truth, and its pursuit and use, is the essence of biblical worldview. And, our authority for truth is the Bible. We aim for students to understand the world through God's eyes, using God's Word as our primary pair of glasses through which we look as we sift ideas and people. Our hope is for every student to see the world the way it really is, which means through God's eyes and Word. There is no reality without God. A claim to see or experience "reality" apart from God and His truth is not really real. God is not only part of reality, but is reality.

We want students to love truth and to know how to find it, in every subject and every relationship. We want them to live a life with God understanding the way things really are, a worldview from God. We want them to fall in love with truth, even as Jesus was full of grace and truth, that each student could become more like Him. All truth, rightly perceived and understood, draws us to God and helps us increasingly know His sovereignty, His power, His mercy. Truth opens our eyes to Him and its pursuit is a worthy one.

Draws to God

A teacher who is doing a great job with biblical worldview will naturally draw students to God.

How can you not be moved by God's mercy when you read *Les Miserable* and the story of Jean Val Jean, giving mercy after receiving mercy from the Bishop? The story shows the power of grace and love.

How can you not be amazed at an all knowing and powerful God who is in control when you study recent work on wave collapse caused by the observer in quantum physics? An approach that helps us understand our limitations of grasping the greatness of God? And, how much bigger He is than us. I do speak over my head on this one.

How can you not know the shallowness and sadness of man apart from God when you consider the wood relief with oil of "Ten Formal Fingers" by Jim Dine? And, feel the hurt of what it must be like to think you are only an impersonal package? The impact of war and a lack of hope in those who don't know God.

The power of a subject understood from and through God's eyes is endless, much as He is. Every subject, pursed rightly, draws a student to God.

Excites Learning

Done well, great biblical worldview grabs students, holds them, and plants seeds deep inside because the teacher is excited to share God through a deep understanding and joy of God's Word and the subject at hand. A teacher's passionate pursuit of learning about subject, life, and God gives students a picture of the joy of learning.

And, as a teacher draws students into this joy, and offers experiences and understanding about the subject as it touches life and truth, students get to experience deep learning. Those students will become short term and life time learners, because they have seen its joy and experienced the process.

Students given knowledge and tools for learning will go to one level. Students who are with great biblical worldview teachers go further, and don't stop. The pursuit of learning is seen as a joy and not a burden, even if it is hard and unreachable at times. Learning isn't about the checklist for a grade, but becomes more. One glimpse of one teacher loving God and subject is enough to make a difference in a life. Many teachers with the same passion and presentation change the world because their students know no ends, only beginnings and steps for learning and pursuing truth and God.

Brings Unity

Fragmentation of disciplines of study and the false separation of secular and spiritual in ideas and life are hallmarks of a society that has no unity of truth, only truth and ideas uncovered piecemeal or studied in isolation. Fragmentation can even happen to us as we separate subjects, unwittingly split what is spiritual and not, and do things like focus on studies primarily to get jobs for students, narrowing the breadth of study and missing the big picture that brings unity and value to life.

Great biblical worldview in every subject recognizes the lordship of Jesus over all creation and the fact that all truth and life hangs together in Him. As Paul says in Colossians 1: "For by him all things were created, in heaven and on earth, visible and invisible, whether thrones or dominions or rulers or authorities—all things were created through him and for him. And, he is before all things, and in him all things hold together."

Unity of truth, the idea that "all truth is God's truth," only happens when there is a framework big enough on which to hang all ideas. Jesus is big enough and the proper framework for bringing together all truth. Science, history, language, health, literature, physical education, Bible, mathematics—all truth finds unity and purpose through a biblical worldview that focuses on Jesus and is rooted in God's Word.

Asks and Answers Questions

Questions can help us think about what we are doing and draw others along. Learning to start with questions helps create life-long learners who seek truth, especially from God's Word. Here are a few questions a teacher might consider while planning and teaching a class with a biblical worldview, questions that students can also help answer as part of the process.

Does the subject and topic have something to say or show about God?

Does God have something to say about the subject?

Does God have something to say about how a class should operate?

Does God have something to say about how a student lives life at school and beyond?

Does the subject point to God and give Him glory, drawing students to Him?

Can we apply biblical truth using the subject and what is learned, like bringing water to the thirsty using chemistry or hope to a dry life from a story?

Great biblical worldview isn't just about asking questions. It is about drawing students into truth of the subject and life, from God's view. Questions are, however, good tools to use with students.

*

Biblical worldview points to Jesus and uses God's Word. It pursues truth which draws students to God. It excites learning and shows a way for all truth to fit together, in Jesus. It uses and answers big questions about life.

It works. We can go there for our students and transform their lives. Every class, every student, all of the time.

THE MODEL FOR BIBLICAL WORLDVIEW

Finding a way to create and keep great biblical worldview for all students in all classes is a formidable task. Thankfully, a simple and powerful foundation using truth from God's Word is available.

The Three Loves.

This section explains the model, what a teacher who loves is like, and the relationship between growing love, passion, and knowledge. And, why each is so important in impacting the lives of students.

4. The Model of the Three Loves

The best biblical worldview happens when there is a living convergence in a teacher of a love for God, a love for subject, and a love for student. It is simple, at one level. But, it is deep, and as true love does, is passionate to know more about the beloved and to give more.

In the classroom with the three loves, in the moment of teaching, with sparkling eyes and reaching hands, the three loves search in the corners of knowledge and heart for just the right example, the most telling fact, the hook that will not let students get away. Truth and life are learned. Love is powerful.

Warning

The danger of analyzing this model, of breaking it apart to understand it, is that we can begin to think that there is a checklist or an answer that will create powerful biblical worldview for every teacher in every place in every time. While the parts of the model which we are getting ready to explain are important to know and use, they are still nothing until put into practice by one teacher at one moment in one class.

The presentation and power in class will be as varied as there are people. A great lesson is hard to replicate in another person because it comes through a living person with a living class with the living Word, not an assembly line with the same part stamped the same way every time. While great lessons accomplish the goals of the curriculum, they do so much more.

Ideas and approaches of great practitioners can be studied and used, but never woodenly, and are more for inspiration and ideation than for replication. The sweet spot of each teacher helps students learn what they are supposed to learn well, with joy, drawing from the passions and depth of the individual teacher when God, subject, and student overlap.

This is a model. Not a checklist.

Love, Simply

Great biblical worldview teachers love God, love students, and love their subject.

The concept is simple enough to learn quickly. But, if done right, it takes a lifetime to discover that you never really get there, that the love and depth of God, subject, and student never ends and is always tantalizing you to go just one more step.

It is deep and worth giving your life to.

That is the joy, this is why we teach. This is why students come to Christian schools. For this passionate draw and depth found in the classrooms of teachers who sincerely love God, love subject, and love student. And, go beyond the fences of a curriculum map to gather everything in the map in their arms, hold it close, and run to new places with students following.

Here is the model, the model of building great biblical worldview that works and transcends time and place.

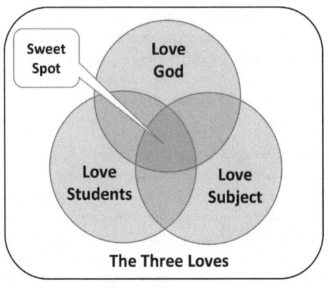

While the parts need to be studied separately to help grow and understand, the three loves must meld back together into something new and living, as the teacher's sweet spot, one place at one time.

The Three Loves Alive in the Teacher

While the model is simple it isn't simply knowing Jesus, understanding students, and earning a degree in a subject area. Great biblical worldview depends on a teacher's love and passion for each of these: Jesus, students, and subject. A love that never ends, that is never satisfied or satiated. The love for each that commandeers a teacher's heart and keeps him or her always pursuing, always learning, always hoping, always growing so that at the moment of the lesson in real time and real life, there is a fresh excitement and joy that draws from an ever increasing body of knowledge buoyed by an ever increasing love for God, students, and subject.

A teacher who loves wants this rich sweet spot now, all of the time, but knows it will take time to learn and grow and that he or she will have only moments of great teaching for a while, before the moments pile on moments and become normal. This teacher treats people well because biblical worldview is about people. This teacher knows that whatever others have learned and do, his or her joy comes from what he or she builds, not comparing to others because the well is deep enough for everyone and different in moment and place.

Honestly, this teacher is sometimes hard to find because he or she just loves doing this with students and is immersed with them, not promoting self, very content to do her thing with students and not boast. This teacher never gives up and knows that there is always more, that even if something derails her heart and work, the best thing is to keep learning and loving and the passion will come back because real love is a commitment not a feeling. This teacher always looks for truth and rejoices in sharing what they find, never ending and always overflowing; she just can't keep it in.

The teacher who loves God, students, and subject has something to offer that others don't. Passion for each keeps the teacher relevant and current, and caring. Students don't care to learn until they know the teacher cares. The impact for learning is greatest when it is obvious the teacher cares not only about the student, but also about the subject and God.

Because of this teacher's love, which is always about an unconditional commitment to others and not just making everyone comfortable and happy, this teacher is something special. This teacher makes a difference, he or she can hardly help it because of the passion that overflows. Even if he or she is a rookie, a genuine and passionate love for God, students, and subject will make him or her valuable. This teacher will always profit a student, and not just be a dead spot in the student's day.

A teacher who doesn't care, who doesn't love outside self, but is content or callous will never be a great biblical worldview teacher. He or she might warm a classroom and keep order, might even have students learn topics from the curriculum map, but will never make an impact worth remembering in the lives of students.

Two of the Three Don't Cut It

To make this I-will-never-forget-what-I-learned impact, the teacher has to have all three loves. A rich biblical worldview does not happen when even one part is left out. There might still be good things going on, in limited ways, but not the power that we look for as we try to gain land in the lives of students and Christian education. Too many educators and too much education only pick two of the three and then hope or pretend to be great Christian education.

Here is what happens when one of the three loves is taken out.

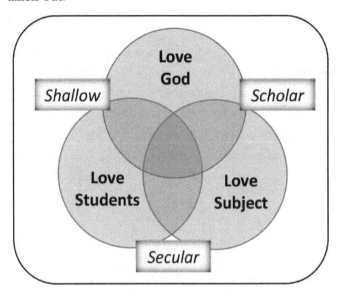

Scholar

If a teacher only loves God and the subject, the teacher is a Scholar. We have a need for Christian scholars. But, not in the classroom teaching and trying to impact the lives of children. This teacher will not reach students, certainly not most of them, because he or she doesn't care about students as a first love, and it will show.

This teacher is not driven to pray for students, to study them, or to keep learning better ways for each to learn. This teacher is not compelled from love to continually learn how to reach and teach students, passionate to know each one and see each child learn about a subject and about the God who created and shaped the subject and the world.

This does not mean the Scholar is a bad person in any way, just that there isn't a love for the student that draws the teacher deeper and deeper into ways to show that love, to communicate, and to impact student lives. It just isn't a passion, and that is okay. But, not okay for a teacher who is in the classroom trying to create great, living, real biblical worldview that touches lives.

Secular

If a teacher only loves the student and the subject, the teacher is Secular. This is not acceptable in a Christian school, yet sometimes I visit classes and have to ask, "How is the class different than the public school down the street?" Higher levels of learning, yes. Positive students and caring faculty, yes. But, the essence of Christian education is to include God, in everything. Even a Christian class with a Christian teacher and Christian students can be secular. If God is left out of the day.

Shallow

And, if a teacher loves students and Jesus, but not subject, it is youth group. Which is of high importance and value. There is a huge place for loving students and loving Jesus and seeing those impact lives, absolutely. It is only "Shallow" related to teaching a school subject, not about impact on life in the most vital area: a relationship with Jesus.

But, youth ministry is not school and Christian school is about being a school and helping students learn subjects and life with God, both. It is Shallow when it comes to learning a subject and doing what a school is supposed to do. A school is called to be a school, and to be the best school that it can be, bringing honor to God not only in our praise to Him, but in the quality of doing what we are meant to do.

A teacher who does not love a subject, has no real heart for it, will do a disservice to accomplishing what a school is supposed to do, and thus disservice to honoring God in work. This person might impact lives for Jesus, and that is absolutely wonderful. But, this teacher does not belong in a school classroom who has a job to do helping students learn subjects.

Satisfied?

Each of these scenarios may have its place. But not in a Christian school that is fulfilling its purpose as a school to give students deep learning that draws students to Jesus and transforms lives. If we don't have teachers who are letting their deep love for God, students, and subject impact lives, are we doing what we are called to do?

I hope the answer is "No," and that we aren't satisfied if any class ever is just taught by a Scholar, is Secular in content, or is Shallow and not doing the work of a school. I hope you have teachers who are living out the sweet spot that comes from a love for God, love for student, and love for subject. I hope we can start sharing your story to help others get there. I hope that you can recall a teacher like this who has taught you so you know and feel the power of learning when you are with a teacher in his or her sweet spot.

Onward up Gaebelein's hill, gaining more ground!

5. Love, Passion, and Knowledge

While the love for God, for students, and for subject must meld together to get to the sweet spot of biblical worldview, there are ways to prepare by taking the model apart and focusing on individual areas. Just like my Plumber friends, training in all parts of their work was important before they put it together to rescue my water bill.

No one walks into a classroom and wings great biblical worldview. A novice can do a pretty good job if there is ability and a love for God, subject, and student, but years of growing and learning add to the power and effectiveness. As long as the teacher continues to be passionate and in love. And, lets that love drive him or her to stay excited about each new group of students, new insights into subject, and a "this is the day the Lord has made, rejoice and be glad in it" sort of fresh joy with God every day.

To understand and grow in biblical worldview that uses the three loves, we need to be clear about the meanings of love, passion, and knowledge and how they affect each other. Love, passion, and knowledge rightly understood, have an important symbiotic relationship that supports deep biblical worldview teaching and learning.

After looking at the meanings and relationship between love, passion, and knowledge, we will look at each of the three loves separately. Always with the end in mind of learning more and then putting them back together.

First, what is biblical love, passion, and knowledge and how do they fit together in biblical worldview?

Love Explained

Sometimes we have this really horrible and convoluted perception of love as feeling, mushy, coming and going, and analyzing, "Am I falling in love?" Of all the words that have been ruined by culture, love has to be at the top of the list. Our world has made love about dreams, rescuing damsels in distress, chocolate, and synonymous with delight or sex. Love is used in so many ways, with so many counterfeits, it is hard to find love the way God loves us and wants us to love.

And yet, God has made it clear that love is important to Him. Loving God and loving people wraps up all the commandments. Love is the end of our instruction, or should be (1 Timothy 1:5). Love guides our truth telling, speaking the truth in love (Ephesians 4:15). Love keeps us from being a noise gong to students, or more likely in class that we sound like the Peanut's teacher who the students hear saying, "wa, wa, wa" (1 Corinthians 13). Jesus says the world will know we are His disciples by the love we have for each other.

Without love for God, student, and subject, powerful biblical worldview will not happen.

But, what is this love like, the love that God wants us to know and have?

What is Love?

God's love, the agapao type, is a lot more about duty than delight. It is a commitment that does what is best for the other person and forgets self. How could God so love the world if His love was based on how He feels? He only would have to take one quick glance and dump us. His love is a commitment.

It is almost always accompanied by sacrifice. A husband who loves his wife like Jesus loves the church gives up something, maybe a golf game, maybe a career, certainly he can't go about his business as if he were the center of the world and still love her. Jesus is the ultimate example of love, giving up His life as a sacrifice. And, certainly not because we are lovely people that would always give Him good feelings by our words and behavior.

Love is about commitment and it is about sacrifice. It is about doing the best for someone who is ugly, nasty, self-important, scared, inept—think Judas when Jesus washed his feet, knowing that Judas was betraying him. That sort of love.

What this Love Does to Teachers

Isn't this what great teachers are like? Because they love, the question for them is "How can I do more?" not "How can I just get done?" These great teachers have to learn to stop themselves for their own sake and for the sake of their families. They have to learn how put on the back thrusters and get out of the black hole of teaching because their love keeps them flitting in and out of being consumed by commitment to students and subject. They have to make sure they aren't Marthas too busy serving and miss the better part that Mary chose.

But, here is what they don't have to do, these teachers who love with God's agapao.

They don't have to be prodded to do professional development. They are always learning and finding ways to love better. They don't have to be forced to try a new idea each quarter and follow top down mandates in their classroom because they have already tried ten, looking for better ways to love students. They don't have to be made to take Bible classes to increase their knowledge of God; their love for Him keeps them constantly wanting to know more.

They are lovers in the best sense, lovers who cling on every word of the beloved and are drawn deeper with a growing love by knowing more. Not only for God, which is a given, but a love that shows in learning more about what they teach and about those young people God has given them, young people with eternity in them, not simple, but fascinating. If the teacher loves.

Choosing to Love

How do we love like that?

Pretty simple. "We love because He first loved us" (1 John 4:19).

We cannot love an agapao love, unconditionally, with commitment and sacrifice, without knowing His love.

Certainly His love on the cross, but also that deep and wide love that fascinates us every day because of Him. A love that makes us fall on our face in unworthiness and weight. A love that makes us leap and sing from the fringes that spill into daily life in surprising ways. If, we keep our eyes open. To love others well, we must dig deeper and deeper into God's love for us.

You know this: we don't feel like loving students every day. We don't feel like loving our subject all the time, "Why did I major in that?" we ask. We don't even feel like loving God all the time. But, that is why an understanding of God's love for us, and that this love is more commitment than feeling, is incredibly important.

Love does not begin with feeling, in fact love often operates contrary to feeling but always for the best of the other person. Often the feeling, the passion, follows love. Especially when we act on our love, because as Bob Goff says, "Love does." And, well, so does James say, "But prove yourself doers of the word, and not merely hearers who delude themselves." And, Paul, "Only do not turn your freedom into an opportunity for the flesh, but through love serve one another." Where your treasure is, there is your heart. What you protect and hold and care for, that is your treasure; it is what you love. The heart, the feeling following. Committed love first, feeling follows.

Which helps so much in the classroom when sometimes you have to look at little Johnny, clinch your teeth, and squeeze out of yourself, "I love him…he is horrible, but I love him…what do I do?"

But, also know that this type of love does not always feel good for the beloved, for the student. Because God's agapao love is about what is best, sometimes it is discipline. Sometimes it is a call home. Sometimes it is a harder assignment. This is strong love, not waiting on feeling, but with deep commitment choosing best, choosing sacrifice, and choosing God's deeper way to love.

The teacher who wants to teach with power must have this type of love.

Two Results of Love

Love has two results, well more I am sure, but two that are critical for teaching with a powerful biblical worldview.

Love leads to passion, the showing of love in emotion.

And, love leads to a deeper knowledge, a depth of understanding that when mixed together with passion creates the elixir of biblical worldview.

Biblical worldview begins with love. It spills into passion and knowledge. In the right hands, it becomes special, a class that fulfills the curricular plan, but goes so much further in the lives of students. Students don't forget these teachers or what they teach by word and by example, actually by their lives.

Let's look more at passion now and its relationship to love.

Passion Extolled

I don't know if you have seen the old *Apollo 13* movie. There is a great scene at the end where all of Mission Control is leaping and laughing and hugging because they have rescued the crew. All but one. The man in charge looks around and quietly sits down in the middle of the celebration. He is no less excited or passionate about what they have done, and maybe even more than the others. But, he shows it differently.

Passion for God, for students, and for subject are necessary. But, passion doesn't show itself the same in all of us. I am like the *Apollo 13* guy who sits down, and you may be, too. Or, you may show your emotions and love in ways that everyone understands, even dancing and skipping when you talk about your God, your subject, or your students.

The Case for Passion

Sometimes the word "passion" scares us because it seems to go hand-in-hand with uncontrolled emotion. But it doesn't have to be that way, it just has to be something that grips us and brings along emotion, even if we keep those emotions behind a calm and stoic face. Emotion is about being human.

If there is no emotion for God, students, or subject, the teacher won't communicate with students in a way that they know is real. Students are drawn to passionate people, who share their hearts and feelings. Feelings, passion, is the heat that boils love for God, for subject, and for students into a new mixture that is powerful and gripping biblical worldview education.

In *On Rhetoric,* Aristotle says that persuasion by a speaker depends on three things. Ethos, the character and integrity of the speaker. Logos, the knowledge and truth of the speaker. And, pathos, the passion and love for the audience, the listener. A teacher with no pathos, no emotion, will not communicate well and is much like the "man without a chest" that C. S. Lewis describes in *Abolition of Man*; this person is empty and questionably human, a human who is just a shell. A person who loves the idea of rescuing humanity like Weston in Lewis's Space Trilogy, but forgets about individuals and what is best for each, real love.

There is nothing wrong with passion, and much lost when we don't feel strongly about our God, our students, and our subject. A teacher with no chest goes through the motions, perhaps following all of the right steps in the latest book on pedagogy for the greater good, but not changing lives.

The Power of Passion

Often we forget that there are three domains of learning in Bloom's taxonomy, not just one. Many educators only know about or think about using the cognitive domain, the domain that focuses on intellectual skills. The cognitive, and its levels of thinking, are important and should be used. But, to many it is the only domain relevant for teaching goals and methods.

The second domain is the affective, the one about feeling. Some have said that all learning begins at the feeling level: if the student doesn't want to learn or isn't interested, there is no learning. That is probably true. Learning goals in the affective domain are as legitimate as the cognitive and needed for students to learn well. How a student feels about a subject or class or God affects learning and should be a part of legitimate lesson planning objectives.

Each year as a principal, I had students complete surveys of all teachers, grades seven through twelve. Twenty statements with a response of "Always" to "Never." And, two open ended questions: "What is one thing the teacher did well?" and "What is one thing to change?" The large majority of students take this seriously and give valuable input for faculty. Students really do know good teaching and learning.

After reading results of around 6,000 inputs a year (900 or so students with seven classes each), one response from the open ended questions was repeated again and again about our great teachers, year after year.

The repeated response: The teacher has passion for the subject and God.

Even the specific word "passion" was often used in open ended questions. Students notice passion and it grabs their attention. A teacher can love, but if it doesn't show somehow in emotion appropriate to that teacher and the situation, students don't see it. Expressing love in passion attracts students and draws students deeper.

For those of you who are more extrovertish, showing your passion tends to be easier. For those of us on the introvertish side, in a world of noise and media, we need to make sure students understand our passions, our deep love showing itself in feeling.

Because I am more like the leader in *Apollo 13*, I needed to help my students and teachers know that certain somewhat mellow words and actions actually came with deep feeling. Whatever your disposition, you need to make sure students know the signals for how you feel, so they understand our hearts. We want our love and its passion to be known, and known the way we intend.

Besides passion, love also results in a growing knowledge of the beloved.

Let's look at knowledge now and its relationship to love and passion.

Knowledge Examined

Great biblical worldview occurs when that sweet spot where love for God, love for student, and love for subject overlap and become something new, something that takes all three parts. Loves that are growing, gaining on truth, and showing in the words and actions of the teacher, in passion.

Love drives passion. Love also desires knowledge. And the three—love, passion, and knowledge—support and affect each other.

The Need for Knowledge

As one of my wise professors, Howard Hendricks, said, "You cannot impart what you do not possess." A teacher must know something. Or, the teacher has nothing to teach. Now, the teacher does not have to know everything, but still must possess a level of knowledge and depth of understanding about God and subject, or he or she will have nothing to say. Teachers who have nothing to impart harm students.

While a teacher without adequate knowledge to impart hurts students, an absence of knowledge can hurt even more in other ways than only missing the content students should learn. Sometimes the content to learn can be found from a book, a video, or other resource even if the teacher does not know the specific item or skill. With access to so much information today, it is possible for a teacher to not know much and still steer students to content.

While a teacher without good knowledge can perhaps direct students to some content, there are three other areas that will not happen without a good and growing knowledge in the teacher. Without good and growing knowledge, the students will not get a passion for the subject, know the value of the subject, nor experience deep learning.

Knowledge and Passion Feed Each Other

A teacher needs a certain level of growing knowledge to have and share a passion for God, a subject, and students. Some knowledge seems necessary before we can love God deeply or a subject well. The more we know, the deeper we love. This is certainly true about God. How can I not love Him more as I better understand His love for me, His glory and grace to me? And, it is true of a growing knowledge of students and subject: knowing more stirs passion and deeper love. Knowledge grows passion.

At the same time, the more I love God with passion, the more I will want to know Him. The more committed in love I am to God, students, and subject, the more I will gain in knowledge because that is what love does. It loves to learn about the beloved. Passion drives knowledge.

So, which comes first? The knowledge or the love and passion? It is a circle, one leads to the other. We can feed it by knowing more or by loving more deeply.

For knowledge to influence love and passion, it cannot be from already chewed food, digested and put in neat paragraphs in a textbook. Textbooks are great for their purposes such as overviews and making sure certain topics are covered, but usually the type of learning that drives increased love and passion comes from things like original sources, life experiences, personal research, or digging into the mine of Scripture for self. The closer to life and origin, the more likely the learner grows in love. This is true of looking at the Bible for yourself, not just reading what somebody else has packaged. It is also true of history and science and math and English and, well, everything. Too much processed knowledge, like processed food, is not healthy.

It isn't all work and no play that makes Jack a dull boy, it is all second hand information that makes him dull.

This is true for the teacher, also. To avoid being dull, he or she must continue to learn, beyond the base knowledge of the subject needed to step into the classroom. A teacher should know basic ideas, but not neglect current journal articles, personal research, following tweets and reading blogs, visiting places and people, reading Shakespeare and not just what somebody says about Shakespeare. Direct, personal engagement in areas of interest create a passion and deeper love and give the teacher something to share with students. Not just the basics, but a zeal for the subject that comes from keeping it fresh in the teacher's life.

Love seeks to know more. Knowing more deepens love.

Knowledge Clarifies Value

A second reason to have a broad knowledge that is growing is to give students perspective. A teacher may not need to know everything, but does need to know what is important for students to learn, what is worth student time and effort. A good understanding of the entire field of study lets the teacher direct learning to the essential and to point students in directions of discovery that are worthy of their time. With overwhelming amounts of information available, what is worth learning? Only a teacher with depth and breadth of a field can help clarify value.

Knowledge Knows Special Places

A few years ago, Dana and I were hiking in the Collegiate Peaks in Colorado, one of our favorite spots. We looked at a trail new to us in a guide book, and the book said it was a delightful trail up a mountain to rushing waters on top. But, a guide from Noah's Ark Whitewater and Adventure Company told us that it was bad, that is was dry and hot and full of uncomfortable switch backs. The guide happened to be our son, to make things worse.

We ignored our son's advice and went with the book. It was pretty bad. I think now that the book must have been written in a previous geological age. It was just as our guide had warned us.

You can easily go in the mountains with a group of friends and not use mountain guides. And, you may have a wonderful time. But, you are also just as likely to miss some of the awesome views, streams, waterfalls, or fields of flowers that were just around the corner. You might get stuck on a trail like we did or go where hundreds of trees fell in a storm and cut off your way (which we also did), so you spend time going places that are hard work and not needed.

A Noah's guide who knows the mountain and is trained well won't take away from your experience, but will add to it. He or she will show you places you might overlook as a casual tripper. Or, help you spend your limited time in beautiful places instead of backtracking because of snow on the trail or wishing your trip was over because of the heat and ugliness.

A teacher needs enough knowledge of the lay of the land in their subject to do the same for students. To take them on good paths, knowing that struggles on hard journeys have value but also suck up the time and energy for bigger things. To point them to trails and peeks around corners that would be missed if the teacher didn't know the big picture and the ways to get in and out. Keeping students from being lost and helping them experience wonder and excitement requires a teacher with knowledge of the subject. Not a need to know everything but a need to guide in and out, get to great places, and keep perspective.

*

Love, God's way, affects and is effected by passion and knowledge. A deepening love results in passion and knowledge, and that passion and knowledge expresses and deepens the love. In some ways, these three are the like the qualities Aristotle used to describe persuasion: Knowledge is the logos, passion is the pathos, and love is the ethos. And, the three are similar to Bloom's three domains. Cognitive, to know, is knowledge. Affective, to feel, is passion. And psychomotor, to do, is love. Love is multifaceted, and much more than the feeling or soft word we are often led to believe in our culture. It is strong and deep and wrapped with knowledge and passion.

Now that we know a little more about love and its relationship with knowledge and passion, let's look at the three loves separately, and how we can grow in each to become great biblical worldview teachers. The love for God, love for student, and love for subject.

GROW THE THREE LOVES

Before the three loves can grow together and create a powerful biblical worldview, each of the loves needs to exist and grow. What can we do to help each along? How can we help each grow so the teacher is alive with passion and has learned deeply enough to have something worth giving the student?

Not forgetting that in the end, these three have to come together to reach the sweet spot of powerful biblical worldview in the classroom.

Let's look at the three loves separately and see how we can help each along.

6. Love for God

Only one thing is big enough to sustain the unbelievably risky and draining work of teaching. And, to take us to deep places with students as they learn about God, subject, and life.

How do we get there? How do we love students? How do we love our subject, a part of the created world? How do we get to the point where we can love students and love subject to be great biblical worldview educators?

The First Love, In Every Way

There is only one way. To teach well begins and ends with a love for God.

Period.

Nothing else will keep us going, day in and day out. Nothing will let a teacher walk into a classroom and create a biblical worldview, in every subject every day for every student. Nothing makes this possible except a love for God.

I know. There is more a teacher needs than "just" to love God. A teacher cannot say, "I love God" so now I can be a teacher. But, the reality is that when the teacher doesn't love God, teaching collapses under the weight of life and ideas. It is not sustainable.

But, if a capable teacher loves God, everything else comes, the person and their pedagogy are stable and lasting. Things will fall in place, not always beautifully in our fallen world and not immediately, but according to His provision and plan.

If we love God the way God says to love Him, the result is a compelling love for people and for living a life that makes a difference in this world. A love for God drives a love for our students. It drives a love and joy for our slice of the world that is ours to redeem, ours to steward, ours to help make kingdom-like, impacting His world with the good works He has prepared ahead.

A person who loves people or loves parts of the world before God, either before in time or in priority, is putting something else in God's place. Not only will this fail because people and things always let you down, but those are idols. If a person or an idea or a classroom or a job or a subject comes first in your life or mine, it is wrongly taking God's place. Idols. Distortion of life. A life out of order with the Creator makes a teacher who has only a distorted view of God and the world—a messed up worldview—to offer students.

We are only worthwhile to students if God is the first love of our lives.

The Results of Loving God

What happens when we love God? We love others because we know and have received His love. We sacrifice self because we understand and have received sacrifice. We impart what we possess.

We fulfill the law. We do what Jesus said. We are empowered. We become less, He becomes more. We become useful. We make a difference.

When we love God we become a person who has something to offer students, a passion for God that each student needs. We also have the power and grace to teach, not from ourselves but by the power of the Holy Spirit who can freely work. We obey Him which allows the Holy Spirit to work, which gives us freedom to love, which makes us useful for His service. We make more of Him, less of ourselves.

The Beating Heart

When we love God, we cannot help but talk about Him. Our students hear and see this love, our first love. But, how does this love for God help us teach with a powerful biblical worldview?

Deuteronomy 6 gives us a pattern, step by step, to take the love for God and have real impact in the lives of children. While it is addressed to parents and a long time ago in Israel, it is equally useful today for those of us who teach children, especially as we partner with parents.

There are three steps. The first step is a love for God in verses 4 and 5. The second step is the bridge between that love and active teaching. The third step is the active teaching life. But, before the three steps, let's look at how Moses begins this section. He looks at the end first, what results this process will have in children's lives. Backwards mapping at its best and a long time before Covey's "start with the end."

The End Result in the Lives of Children

"That you and your son and grandson might fear the Lord your God, to keep all His statutes and His commandments which I command you, all the days of your life, and that your days may be prolonged. O

Israel, you should listen and be careful to do it, that it may be well with you and that you may multiply greatly, just as the Lord, the God of your fathers, has promised you, in a land flowing with milk and honey" (Deuteronomy 6:2 and 3).

Isn't this what we want for our students? To listen and act on what they hear so that their "days may be prolonged" and that "it may be well with" them. That they may fear God, in all of its rich, awesome, emotional, and relational ways and to keep His commands, to live a life in a way that gives them the best and fullest life possible, walking with the Creator according to how creation works and the Creator's plan. Shalom. That is our aim.

Wouldn't it be a blessing for you and your students if things go well, if there is growing, and enjoyment of Him and His blessings? Can you imagine a classroom like that? A home? A life? A society?

How? How do we take our slice of the Kingdom and use God's process to help redeem it?

Step One: Love God

Israel is told, "Hear, O Israel! The Lord is our God, the Lord is one! You shall love the Lord your God will all your heart and with all your soul and with all your might? (Deuteronomy 6:4 and 5).

Impacting the lives of children starts by knowing who God is and loving God with our entire being.

I don't know how to expand on that or explain it better. We each need to come to grips with where we are in our totality of love for God. All of me, all of my heart, my inner being, my physical being. Do I love God that way? That question should be our barometer morning, noon, and night, and in between. Before we consider anything else about ourselves. How am I doing in my love for God?

Step Two: The Bridge

"These words which I am commanding you today shall be on your heart" (Deuteronomy 6:6).

What does it mean to have God's words "on your heart"? How do you make that happen? This is the critical middle step, the bridge between loving God in verses 4 and 5, and teaching children, which comes up in verses 7 through 9.

To understand what it means to have God's words "on your heart," let's start with what Moses said shortly before he dies, in Deuteronomy 32:46: "Take to your heart all the words which I am warning you today, which you shall command your sons to observe carefully, even all the words of this law. For it is not an idle word for you; indeed it is your life. And by this you will prolong your days in the land, which you are about to cross the Jordan to possess."

When Moses says to take the words to heart, they are to be observed carefully, do what they say. And, this is no small thing. It is life. Being on your heart has a lot to do with obedience.

Look in chapter 11 of Deuteronomy as Moses has more to say about love and heart.

11:1: "You shall therefore love the Lord your God, and always keep His charge, His statutes, His ordinances, and His commandments."

Love for God is directly linked to doing the things God says, obedience.

11:13: "It shall come about, if you listen obediently to my commandments which I am commanding you today, to love the Lord your God and to serve Him with all your heart and soul, that He will give the rain for your land in its season…"

Again, obedience. Love and active serving are both commanded, with our whole being.

And, Moses says in 11:16 "Beware that your hearts are not deceived, and that you do not turn away and serve other gods and worship them."

It is a matter of heart, yours and mine. The choice to have God's words on them, or to have our hearts deceived. No middle ground. Going from love to making a difference in teaching is always about our hearts, and then student hearts. We choose to have God's words on our hearts or to be deceived, and that choice makes all of the difference in our lives and our value as a teacher who can teach with a biblical worldview.

The concept of love tied to obedience plays throughout the Bible. Obedience as a response to God's love to us and as part of our love for Him. Listen to Jesus in John's Gospel.

In John 14: "He who has My commandments and keeps them is the one who loves Me; and he who loves Me will be loved by My Father, and I will love him and will disclose Myself to him."

Keeping God's commandments, not as duty, but as a response to His love, shows—and in fact is—love to God.

Jesus links obedience and loving people in John 11 beginning in verse 12: "This is My commandment, that you love one another, just as I have loved you. Greater love has no one than this, that one lay down his life for his friends. You are My friends if you do what I command you."

Loving people, and specifically for us, students, is the result of loving God and having His Words on our heart, changing our hearts.

To obey doesn't sound glamourous, but it is powerful. Love. Obey. We are each different, and in this obedience the Holy Spirit can take each teacher's heart and do all the things the Holy Spirit does: lead, teach, guide, open eyes, empower, convict, comfort. Our obedience out of love for God and into love for students lets the Spirit work and gives the teacher something living that students catch and see, a life that sees God in all of living including the subject and the students.

This love for God and a changed heart makes possible the next step, active and life changing teaching.

Step Three: Active Teaching

"You shall teach them diligently to your sons and shall talk of them when you sit in your house and when you walk by the way and when you lie down and when you rise up. You shall bind them as a sign on your hand and they shall be as frontals on your forehead. You shall write them on the doorposts of your house and on your gates" (Deuteronomy 6:7-9).

Teach, talk through the day, make the words on your heart evident when people see you, make them evident when someone comes to your place. When we love God and do what He says, this happens. And, it makes a difference in lives. Students hear and see that God is real and a part of life, as we teach, talk, and show Him through our days with them. This is the active teaching and talking we do that impacts lives and is possible because of our changed heart.

The education we offer children should be whole, encompassing everything about our time with them and putting God in his rightful place in all we do and say, every moment from bell to bell and overflowing in the hall and wherever else we go. This is a natural outgrowth of the teacher who loves God with everything and has a changed heart from His words. It will not happen if a teacher does not love God and have a changed, and changing, heart. Biblical worldview is about all of life, the wholeness of children and teachers, and seeing the subject and life from God's view. An outgrowth of loving God well.

I would be negligent if I didn't point out a warning and an opportunity that follows in Deuteronomy 6. A warning that is applicable for many of us and our schools. And a life changing opportunity.

The Warning

"Then it shall come about when the Lord your God brings you into the land which He swore to your fathers, Abraham, Isaac, and Jacob, to give you, great and splendid cities which you did not build and houses full of good things which you did not fill, and cisterns which you did not dig, vineyards and olive trees which you did not plant, and you eat and are satisfied, then watch yourself, that you do not forget the Lord who brought you from the land of Egypt, out of the house of Slavery" (Deuteronomy 6:10-19).

Moses goes on to tell Israel to fear the one real God, that He is jealous. And, if they don't fear God and follow His commandments, God will be angry and act on that anger. If they do fear God and obey, things will go well.

Israel, like us, is in danger of forgetting God as they enjoy the good things that others did for them. Many of us find ourselves in schools where a lot of work has been done already to make our schools places that are good. Not perfect maybe, but places that we did not build and in which we enjoy the foundation and blessings of others. Things we did not make but benefit from.

When things are good, as Moses said, it is easy to forget who made them good and go about our days leaving God out. All good things are from Him. If we are blessed and benefit from things we did not do, we should be especially careful to put God in His rightful place. It is so easy to forget. Thus the warning and one for us, especially when things are good.

An Opportunity

"When your son asks you in time to come, saying, 'What do the testimonies and the statutes and the judgments mean which the Lord our God commanded you?' then you shall say to your son, 'We were slaves…'" (Deuteronomy 6:20-15).

When we have abundant lives and active classrooms like this chapter describes, where we talk about God and unabashedly keep Him obvious to all who enter, we will have "teachable moments" when students finally ask and really want to know what this God is all about. These are powerful times.

Not all students will respond as we go day to day, but many times and sometimes years later, students will finally say, "What does this mean?" Then you will tell the great things you have seen, not old stories but stories about a living God in your life. As Israel would tell about being slaves and being free, because they experienced it, be ready to tell students about your own rescue by God and how they can be redeemed as well.

And, God's abundance and grace in the life you see and know.

Look for these special moments when students ask. They will come if you are faithful to love God and have His words on your heart.

Loving God, putting His words on your heart, and then talking and living a life with God and through God to students. That is pure biblical worldview. That becomes great biblical worldview in class when combined with a love for students and a love for subject.

*

I love this Facebook post by one of my teachers. "It is back to school time. I can no longer avoid the ending of sweet July. The first way I prepare to teach teenagers has nothing to do with the English curriculum or standards. First, I prepare my heart."

She gets it. And, even though she is a young teacher, her love for God, student, and subject make her a powerful English teacher with an equally powerful biblical worldview. She impacts lives.

Growing Love for God

How do we love Him better, with a love that changes us and gives us something vital for students?

There are many disciplines and approaches, but let me land on this one for now because it seems to be the one most difficult and, perhaps, absent in our culture. Listen to A. W. Tozer in *The Pursuit of God*, ironically from 1948 but could have been written today:

"The idea of cultivation and exercise, so dear to the saints of old, has now no place in our total religious picture. It is too slow, too common. We now demand glamour and fast-flowing dramatic action. A generation of Christians reared among push buttons and automatic machines is impatient of slower and less direct methods of reaching their goals. We have been trying to apply machine-age methods to our relations with God. We read our chapter, have our short devotions and rush away, hoping to make up for our deep inward bankruptcy by attending another gospel meeting or listening to another thrilling story told by a religious adventurer lately returned from afar."

"The tragic results of this spirit are all about us. Shallow lives, hollow religious philosophies, the preponderance of the element of fun in gospel meetings, the glorification of men, trust in religious externalities, quasi-religious fellowships, salesmanship methods, the mistaking of dynamic personality for the power of the Spirit: these and such as these are the symptoms of an evil disease, a deep and serious malady of the soul."

*

Your love for Jesus leads to:
Studying Him
Knowing Him
Talking about Him
He is on your mind
Following Him
Pursuing Him
Excitement about life with Him
Talking to Him
Listening to Him
What else?

7. Love for Student

We love because He first loved us. Love of God is first, foundational, and foremost. Without a love for God we will love students only in part or in the shallows, not all the time and not deeply. The only way we can love all of time and deeply is to love God and know His love for us. And, in spite of us.

If love for a student or students is not happening, the first place to look is how our love for God is going, not at the student's issues. Nothing stops love the way God does it and wants us to do it. That doesn't mean it always works or is reciprocated. That doesn't happen for God either. But, we can only love students well if we know we are loved by God and we love God.

The Choice of Commitment

Love for a student has nothing to do with the student. It has only to do with our commitment to him or her, to do what is best with a love that God gives. It doesn't matter if a group of students is lovely or nice or easy to love. That may change our approach, as it should, but it should not change our motivation to love them and their understanding that we are committed to them, even in discipline and required hard work. It is about what is best, in God's eyes, for the students. And the student. Love really is always about an individual, even when we are making group decisions.

Love for students is our motivation. It is why we do what we do, or it should be. There is nothing that will sustain a teacher like love for students. And, nothing that will be more obvious to students when it is absent. We can have bad days and good days, days we feel like loving and days we don't. Students get that. But, it never means we stop loving. It is not based on feeling, it is based on commitment rooted in what God has done for us.

Depravity and Deeper Love

I am a sinner. A pretty bad one. And, you know what? You are, too. Realizing the depth of our sin and sins and God's grace to rescue us from them helps us go to sinners and love them. If we are struggling with loving a student, we probably need to spend more time considering our own depravity, the horribleness of being a filthy rag, deceitfully wicked.

Then take some time looking at whom Jesus hung out with in the Gospels. He spent his choice time with the broken, the hurting, and the obvious sinners. The self-righteous didn't need Him, or at least they didn't think so. What student are you going to make sure you love, if you are trying to love like Jesus did? What class are you going to commit to, if you are loving like Jesus did? The horrible one last period on Friday or the group that does everything you tell them, early in the day?

What Loving Students Does to Teachers

This love for students compels us to do all we can to reach and touch and grow them. It compels us to learn how students learn, so we can make a difference. It drives us to plan lessons better, to understand pedagogy, to know if students are getting it or not, and then to adjust so they do. Love for students makes us do all we can to get to know each one, to ask questions about their lives, to hang out with them at lunch and at ball games, or to find other ways to understand each one better so we can help each one learn.

Love for students compels us to many other actions, but here are three that stand out.

Truth

Love compels us to help students learn truth from God's eyes. Any good teacher can teach your subject, but only a teacher in love with God and students can impact lives for eternity in a good way. Love for students is why we do all we can to live God before them and with them, to make sure that our subject is learned in light of eternal truth for God's glory. Love compels us to the richest and truest truth we can give them and hopes they are inspired to use the truths of our subject and of God in their lives. At least to know God is real and involved in life, in our subject and in all we do in class and out.

Best

Love compels us to do our best for students. We will always fail, if we are a good teacher, because our hopes and goals are for more. But, we always do our best with what God has given us, in resources and intellect, in culture and in life. David used things he had and knew to beat Goliath. We can pick up stones we already have and use them, too. We don't need to wait for the bigger and better to love and teach a biblical worldview. Use what we know and have. Our best starts now, not when everything is perfect and together.

Content

Besides love for students being our motivation, love is also part of the content that we want students to learn. If students can see the love we have for God and the love we have for our subject, they will more likely catch the same loves. They will at least try to understand what makes a teacher so different, so passionate. A seed in some, a fertilizer in others, a greenhouse for all.

We not only need to love students, but they need to know we love them. There is a difference, and a significant one. I know some fine teachers who sincerely love students but struggle in having a student feel that love. It is not enough to say, "I love you." Love is an action, a commitment. We have to show our love in ways students understand.

Benefits of Loving Students

I almost don't want to point out the benefits that come when we love students. We should love no matter what. But, there are some things that often happen from the power of unconditional love.

Trust

If students know you care, that you love them, they will do almost anything for you. They will trust you. They will accept discipline well. They will work hard. They will believe you, or at least give you a chance, when you talk about God's goodness or God's view of your subject which might be different than their current views of life. If you want to make serious impact in lives, you have to make sure students know you love them so they will trust you.

Learning

I always enjoy when research supports what God says, which accurate research does. My friend Kevin Washburn writes about some research, "Memory construction—and therefore learning—includes emotional data. In fact, emotion drives and enables learning. It focuses a student's attention, allows her to find meaning, and feeds motivation." (Kevin Washburn, *The Architecture of Learning*, 2010. Clerestory Press, pages 41 and 42.) Knowing you are loved is a compelling and powerful feeling that helps students learn. Feeling loved is a gift that Christian teachers should give students.

Discipline

Some of my greatest successes have been when I expelled students and they hugged me and thanked me. They knew I cared, that I loved them, and was committed to the best for them. That I had done all I could for them, no stone unturned. But, that I now had no option, they had left me with no choice. They knew I wanted to continue a relationship and it hurt me not to. A student who knows he or she is loved is a changed person, if not now, later. There is way too much conditional love in our world, based on performance and standards. Love the way God loves makes a difference.

Communication

One of the benefits of God becoming a man in Jesus is helping us understand His love for us. The incarnation is worth considering when you are thinking about how to show love to students. Going where they are, spending time with them outside of class, taking moments in class to share your life or talk to individuals—invading their lives enough that they know you love, so when you say the words or act on it, they understand better and accept it. There is truth in "earn the right to be heard."

Bridges

You know this I am sure, but when parents know you love their children, they are so much more eager to work with you. They know you have a common goal and commitment. You may not agree on some things, but knowing your love for their children makes the paths smoother and the bonds stronger. And, the best way to let them know you love their child? Make sure the student knows; they will tell their parents. Then it isn't just you saying it, it is real to them.

Two Ways to Love Students Better

Besides increasing your love for God and your understanding of your own sin, let me give two suggestions to help you love students better. And, one warning.

First, know them better

Just as knowing God better helps us love Him more deeply, getting to know students better helps you love them. Certainly the more you know, the easier it is to communicate and for them to know you care by your interest and knowledge. But, it goes deeper. When you discover that a child just spent the weekend with a harsh and unbelieving parent, it may increase your commitment to her as well as your communication. When you know a child's mom has cancer, you may find it easier to discipline in a way that communicates your love. When you know the student has small epileptic seizures, it may be easier to commit to praying for him. Knowing helps loving. As long as we don't think we are better than them, but know that we are just as broken, needy, and sinful. And that we can offer God's love and grace to the child as we help him or her learn about the world from God's eyes.

Second, pray for them

A second way to increase your love is an idea I am stealing from Guy Doud, the 1986 National Teacher of the Year and speaker of "Molder of Dreams." I will never forget the simple thing he did that I have seen teachers do since then that makes a huge difference in reaching students, in loving them and their learning well. Guy simply would sit in a student's desk before the day started and pray for the student. If you have time, you can sit in several. Or, you can do that after school. We all have time to sit in one desk each day, for one minute, and pray, don't we? This is powerful, and simple. And, helps us love students better. (And, for administrators, sneak in a teacher's room after hours and do the same; it works.)

The Easy to Love

Last, a warning. It is really easy to love some students because they love us back. Or, because they do all the right things. Watch that our commitment goes to all students, not just those easy to love. Maybe go through your list of students and consider your commitment, unconditionally to each one and where you are. And, ask yourself, does every student know I love him or her?

Be a little careful about loving students who always do the right thing. Obviously, all students need love, those choosing right and those who aren't. But, be careful that our affirmations for doing right don't lead a student to think that doing right is the answer to getting love, or to living life. They need to know that they are loved no matter what. While we value doing right, we also value them and want to help them in a walk with God that is real, in its victories and failures.

Consider God's standard on how people will know we are Christians. Jesus says in John 13 that they will know we are His disciples by the love we have for each other. He did not say doing the right things. Now, I think students should do the right things. But, if it is easier to show love to those doing right, those students may learn that following certain standards is more important than learning to love others as Jesus said.

Often, like Jesus, those who love well are misunderstood, by the world and by God's people.

Teachers who love like Him may also be misunderstood.

*

Your love for your students leads to:
Studying them
Knowing them
Talking about them
They are on your mind
Going where they are
Pursuing them
Excitement about them
What else?

8. Love for Subject

Love for God and love for students are foundational to powerful biblical worldview. They make the Christian school distinctive. They are what make us different than the non-Christian school down the street. Real, living biblical worldview that impacts students does not happen unless a teacher loves God and loves students. And, is driven in that love to know more about each and to help students see a world, a worldview, with God in its center in all things and through God's eyes.

Love for God and for students fit easily with God's Word, with love for God always tops so that we are not idol worshippers. God and people are eternal, so they are elevated in their value in terms of why we do what we do and our focus. When living a life guided by priorities, these are one and two. And, they are the first and second steps for a great biblical worldview teacher. If you aren't loving God and loving students, class will be a façade of real life and what students could learn from you. So, these two loves are not to be overlooked or considered something we do when we have time, they are who we should be all of the time.

But, what about love three, the love for subject?

Obviously, love for subject doesn't carry the same weight as the clear statements from the Bible to love God and love people.

Or does it?

The Case for Loving Your Subject

Let's consider a few passages that might influence our view of loving our subject.

"Finally, brethren, whatever is true, whatever is honorable, whatever is right, whatever is pure, whatever is lovely, whatever is of good repute, if there is any excellence and if anything worthy of praise, dwell on these things" (Philippians 4:8). This passage opens the door, not just suggesting but commanding the focus of our minds on topics that fit well in what we want students to learn. Look at the list. They are the ideas we want students to know from each of our subjects. To teach students what is true and excellent in history or mathematics is what we do.

And, God tells us to spend time there.

Or, this, section from Colossians 1:16 and 17: "For by Him all things were created, both in the heavens and on earth, visible and invisible, whether thrones or dominions of rulers or authorities—all things have been created through Him and for Him. He is before all things, and in Him all things hold together."

There is no split between secular and spiritual, all things are wrapped up in Jesus. All subjects should be boldly pursued, doing our school thing, knowing that in the end if done right, they are about Him and the study of them should bring students to Him.

Continuing in Colossians 2:1-5: "For I want you to know how great a struggle I have on your behalf and for those who are at Laodicea, and for all those who have not personally seen my face, that their hearts may be encouraged, having been knit together in love, and attaining to all the wealth that comes from full assurance of understanding, resulting in a true knowledge of God's mystery, that is Christ himself, in whom are hidden all the treasures of wisdom and knowledge" (2:1-5).

Wow. All the treasures of wisdom and knowledge are hidden in Christ. As we study and look at subjects, we should be treasure seekers, anticipating a discovery in our subject that brings us to Him. And, knowing that apart from Christ, we will not discover those treasures of wisdom and knowledge.

Mark Noll, in *Jesus Christ and the Life of the Mind*, explains the high value of studying different subjects. Here is a small part of his comment: "The claims are striking and bear repeating. The apostle says, in effect, that if we study anything in the realms of nature or the realms of the spirit, we study what came into existence through Jesus Christ. Likewise, if we study human interactions or spiritual-human interactions (thrones, dominions, rulers, powers), we are studying realms brought into existence by Jesus Christ. If our study concerns predictability, uniformity, regularity, we are working in the domains of the one who is 'before all things, and [in whom] al things hold together.' If our study concerns beauty, power, or agency, it is the same, 'for God was pleased to have all his fullness dwell in him.' And, if we succeed to any degree, we are only following after Jesus Christ, 'in whom are hidden all the treasures of wisdom and knowledge'." (Eerdmans, 2011, page 28.)

The whole world is understood through Christ, and knowing it better helps us understand Him. Great biblical worldview teachers do this, they know their subject so well and Christ so well that they wrap the two together, always with the Bible as the authority, but with joy of learning more about the Creator and His creation.

And, to affirm the value of study and the unity of all in Christ, let's hear from Frank Gaebelein again: "We must recognize, for example, that we need teachers who see their subjects, whether scientific, historical, mathematical, literary, or artistic, as included within the pattern of God's truth. It is one thing to take for ourselves the premise that all truth is God's truth. It is another thing to build upon this premise an effective educational practice that shows the student the unity of truth and that brings alive in his heart and mind the grand concept of a Christ who 'is the image of the invisible God,' by whom 'all things were created,' who 'is before all things,' and by whom 'all things consist,' or hold together."

And, he follows with, "Once more, then, we set down the premise: All truth is God's truth. Whereupon we must conclude that Christian education has a holy obligation to stand for and honor the truth wherever it is found...To be sure, revealed truth, as stated in the Word of God and known through Christ, is of higher importance than natural truth. But the latter is also within the pattern of God's truth" (*The Pattern of God's Truth*, page 23).

It does seem that that the mind pursuing the bigness of God in His special revelation of Scripture and His general revelation of the created world are good things. Things worthy of our time, and our hearts since all things studied well and deeply should point to and bring Glory to God.

That is the task of the great biblical worldview teacher.

And, it only happens if a love for God, love for students, and love for subject drive the teacher to deeper understanding, knowing each better, and falling in love daily. Sharing that passion and heart, life to life with students so they know God and His world, through God's eyes, with awe and joy.

The Weight of Loving Your Subject

So, does loving your subject carry the same weight as the clear statements from the Bible to love God and love people?

A clear answer: "Yes." And, "No."

The weight of loving your subject is a heavy one. By priority, God is first. People second. But, a life well lived doesn't often have to go to priorities to plan time and choose between those things of value. A life well lived, except for moments, is able to live out all three priorities, and more, and make them all fit. That is the nature of a person managing life well, to be able to fulfill priorities in life and seldom have to decide between them. Because, all are happening in a healthy life.

But, the management of that healthy life for a teacher is a different story.

How do we fit love for subject in a busy life? How do you do that and not spend more time, and potentially take away from other priorities. Already we know that a love of God is the beginning point to be a great biblical worldview teacher. And, love of student needs to happen.

There is a way to love your subject more without spending more time (assuming you are spending some time already). It is a shift, an attitude, an approach change. Not more time, but a different focus to build and keep that love for subject.

Let's assume you know the basics of your subject, that when you look at a standard textbook, you get it. You may not remember everything, but you know where the parts fit and you are familiar with the big ideas and the parts. For a trained educator, this should be the case. If not, there is work to be done either before the class begins in the year, or as you go.

If you have this basic understanding, great. This is a minimal background needed, which if you don't have, will take more time to get.

Then, if you have the basic knowledge, how do you fall in love regularly with your subject so that you have a passion for it and can share that passion with students, especially from God's perspective?

You cannot impart what you don't possess. How do you get a joy and excitement without spending inordinate amounts of time?

Ten Ways to Keep Your Love Fresh

How do you keep love fresh? The ten ideas here work for any love. You can pick and choose some that work for you. Most don't take more time, just a different approach.

Commit

First, is a commitment to that thing or person. That is at the heart of love, God's way. Do you have a commitment? Make it. Doors will open in surprising ways.

Act

What are you doing for that thing or person? Notice I did not say how do you feel? Feelings often follow, after the commitment and acting in love. What actions can you take, even small, out of a commitment?

Pray

Certainly for a person, that you might love him or her well. But, why not for your subject and your work? Pray that God will give you a heart for it, if it is what you are to do. Pray that He will show you insights into Him through it. And, insights from Him and His Word about your subject. Pray that you will be surprised. Awed. Amazed. By something, little things that you have not noticed before or that He brings to your path.

Notice

Lift your head up, look around as you go through your day. Put yourself in a position mentally or physically where you can be surprised. What have you not seen before? Look from a different view point, through someone else's eyes. What would an unbeliever want to know about your subject? What does Julie sitting in the back row see and think when you start your lesson.

Question

They don't have to be profound. Drop a note to parents of students and ask them what they would like to know about your subject. This might amaze and inspire you. Ask Facebook friends what it is about nouns and adjectives that excites them. They will think you are weird, but it would be fun. Be playful. Write the top expert an email and ask what she thinks a student should know, the one thing. Have your students do these things so you don't have to spend the time yet get the benefit. And, so does the student.

Remember

When the bride and king in Song of Solomon are having trouble, the friends ask the bride, "What kind of beloved is your beloved?" Remembering what you originally loved, enjoyed, what pleased you, what caught your interest—remembering those things can bring back your love and help restore feelings of passion.

Anticipate

Expect to be amazed. Jeremiah 33:3 says, "Call to Me, and I will answer you, and I will tell you great and mighty things, which you do not know." God wants to awe us with Himself and His creation. Ask Him. Then expect it. In faith. God will show you.

Consider this from Job: "The departed spirits tremble under the waters and their inhabitants. Naked is Sheol before Him, and Abaddon has no covering. He stretches out the north over empty space and hangs the earth on nothing. He wraps up the waters in His clouds, and the cloud does not burst under them. He obscures the face of the full moon and spreads His cloud over it. He has inscribed a circle on the surface of the waters at the boundary of light and darkness. The pillars of heaven tremble and are amazed at his rebuke. He quieted the sea with His power, and by His understanding He shattered Rahab. By His breath the heavens are cleared; His hand has pierced the fleeing serpent. Behold, these are the fringes of His ways; and how faint a word we hear of Him! But His mighty thunder, who can understand?"

"The fringes of His ways." Be in awe, be amazed. We see only the fringes, and they are almost too much for us to carry or understand. Are you amazed at God's fringes He lets you see in your world of work, your subject? They are there, His awesomeness is there peeking out, waiting for you to notice. Expect them, look for them.

Tidbits

Try some little, practical things. Follow tweets of people in your subject, look at the random ideas. Have students take turns bringing in one item from media every day that either shows God's hand in your subject or how your subject can help understand God better. Read random magazine articles. Do a Google search of a word in the scholarly section and see what comes up. Use the *Encyclopedia of Bible Truths* that ACSI publishes. Look up a book on Amazon and see what other books people buy or read the comments from those who ranked it with a 3. Browse a section of your topic at a library, looking for random, unnoticed books. Look for a Ted talk on your subject. Ask weird questions on search engines, like "Why did Dickens write about poverty?" Caring for the poor is biblical, was that his reason and how does it fit with biblical worldview? (Just looked, supposedly "Because he experienced it as a child and was terrified of it the rest of his life. He was able to write out of his fears and disgust from first-hand knowledge." Did Literature teachers know that?)

Feel

Allow yourself to feel. Slow down for three minutes
and let yourself be affected by a story, a picture, a
verse, or a person. Passion and feeling won't come if
you don't give it a little time to sink in. you might have
to plan times to let yourself feel.

Purpose

Be purposeful. When you write lesson plans for the
week, create a spot in them for something new you
have learned or felt about your subject. Put it on your
to do list. No big deal, just be intentional and keep
loving your subject in front of you. It will happen. And,
you will have something special to share with students.

*

Your love for your subject leads to:
Studying it
Knowing it
Talking about it
It is on your mind
Using it
Pursuing it
Excitement about it
What else?

WHAT'S NEXT?

My hope is that we create a dialogue and ask questions to help Christian school education move forward in biblical worldview for all students, all of the time, in all subjects. Our distinctive and our hope.

If we believe teachers should love God, love subject, and love students to be great biblical worldview teachers, we may need to change hiring, firing, and professional development of teachers. If there is validity to the three loves, it should make a difference in what we do.

Time and Encouragement

First, there needs to be time and encouragement to help teachers put the three loves together as part of their class preparation. It is okay to focus on the three loves separately and to analyze, but they must be brought together as teacher's plan and prepare for their classes, in a living and fresh union of the three loves for each teacher. Teachers should write down in plans ways to show love of God, subject, and students.

Time, reflection, practice, encouragement, and studying the three loves helps this sweet spot happen. Maybe we just start by asking each other, "Did you have any sweet spots this week?" and listen to the stories. We make the idea part of our culture's conversation, keeping it alive and active. We make sure that the teacher has time to consider how he or she is doing in the three loves and how to move forward personally. And, how we all can support that progress. We need to keep giving teachers the tools and books and training for specific biblical worldview practices, but make sure that each is ready for those tools because of his or her love for God, students, and subject.

Permission to Love

Second, teachers need clear permission to love, the way God does, to be encouraged to let the three loves come through them. I know teachers who hold back because they have been taught that their lives are not part of the curriculum. They need to know that great biblical worldview depends on their lives overflowing for God, students, and subject. They need to not only have clear permission, but know that love is expected.

Practices that Support the Loves

Third, specific practices like hiring, firing, teacher readiness, professional development, and evaluation should support the three loves.

The hiring process should dig deeply into the reality of the loves. A teacher's readiness to teach will be based as much, or more, on the three loves than on typical teacher training topics of lesson planning and classroom management.

If the three loves are essential, we cannot keep teachers on staff who cannot or will not learn to love God, students, and subject well. Ways to move them to other roles or to another school or occupation are essential if we have done all we can to help them. Our commitment is first to the students, anyone or anything that cannot or will not become the best for them needs to be replaced.

Professional development should take on new focus and opportunity. "Spiritual life" of faculty, often thought to be a topic for outside of school, becomes a professional growth need and rightfully a part of professional development time and money. Likewise, developing love for students and subjects. Maybe the best professional growth for an individual teacher is a day at the park with a Bible and God and a notebook, costing only a substitute for the day. Maybe it is watching a great biblical worldview teacher in another department or school. Maybe identify your best biblical worldview teachers and ask them where they and others need to grow. You might be surprised. And, it might be simple and easy to do. It will be good to involve them.

Encouragement and evaluation of faculty may need to go a fundamentally different direction. Teachers and school leaders learn to help each other love better, as a part of the imbedded conversation and goal. Evaluation of the three loves, their use, and their results becomes a part of helping teacher

Taking the Land

"There remains much land to be taken" in creating true biblical worldview. "We have had a great deal to say about God-centered, Bible based education. But in practice we are not doing nearly enough of it."

It will only be enough when every student learns all of the time from teachers who create a powerful and rich biblical worldview. It is who we are, our uniqueness and our value we offer.

With well-prepared troops who love God, love students, and love subject we can take the land. Teachers, with a capital T, will take the tools we have, hold the line, and move up. It is about hiring and growing teachers who love well, God's way. The Plumber, not the wrench.

Teachers. Who love well.

By God's grace.

ABOUT THE AUTHOR

Christian school education claimed Joe's focus since seminary where Howard Hendricks showed him the value and power of first hand Bible study used in all parts of life, especially education. And, Ken Gangel showed him the value of Christian schools and doing things right.

Joe served as Head and Principal at Cedar Valley Christian for fourteen years and nine years as an administrator at historic Wheaton Academy. Then, nine years as Upper School Principal of middle school and high school at Little Rock Christian, each earning National Blue Ribbon recognition. In his last two years, the high school was selected as one of the "Best 50 Christian High Schools in America."

Rooted Schools ministry helps Christian schools and the people in them to flourish, with a bent to look at God's Word first for "how we do what we do" in operations, practices, and pedagogy. While we love to study current practice in business, education, and psychology, we like to ask first: "Does Scripture have something to say about how we do what we do?"

Follow us at RootedSchools.org for fresh insights and help to grow your school and the people in them.